tours, variously

Also by
Drew McEwan

If Pressed

repeater

tours, variously

poems by

Drew McEwan

Talonbooks

Talonbooks
9259 Shaughnessy Street, Vancouver, British Columbia, Canada V6P 6R4
talonbooks.com

Talonbooks is located on xʷməθkʷəy̓əm, Sḵwx̱wú7mesh, and səlilwətaɬ Lands.

First printing: 2025

Typeset in Jenson
Printed and bound in Canada on 100% post-consumer recycled paper

Cover illustration: *Untitled* by K. MacNeil

Talonbooks acknowledges the financial support of the Canada Council for the Arts, the Government of Canada through the Canada Book Fund, and the Province of British Columbia through the British Columbia Arts Council and the Book Publishing Tax Credit.

Library and Archives Canada Cataloguing in Publication

Title: tours, variously : poems / Drew McEwan.
Names: McEwan, Drew, author.
Identifiers: Canadiana 20250189453 | ISBN 9781772016871 (softcover)
Subjects: LCGFT: Poetry.
Classification: LCC PS8625.E932 T68 2025 | DDC C811/.6—dc23

for Kit

The separation that is concretized through the intimacy of the [building] outlines new relations with the elements.

—EMMANUEL LEVINAS

Totality and Infinity: An Essay on Exteriority, translated by Alphonso Lingis (1969)

You are now touring actively.
You have responsibilities.

—*Information for Docents* (1971)

a tour, variously

I brace another entryway within a room.

You frame the performance of a beginning.

To live among uncertain property:
another's bare life.

I replace a corner, an association of walls.

You un-touch a past, scan a dispersal.
A line. A span.

A room's weight buttressed against irreconcilable walls.

Alive to yourselves, you distribute
natural spaces, built bodies.

To depart augurs a wager.

Surety echoes into austerity.

Affect impersonal.

As I step, and you step behind me,
notice comfort. Notice discomfort.

You are neither. I guide regardless.

Matter below counts upward.

A sequence to denote a conceited gravity.

You replace half-built concurrences,
                    blueprints of other rooms you've known.

These I will buttress as we build a tour together.

Who among you has visited these four walls before?
Raise your hand.

Dust accumulation, a categorical process.

Reorder architecture
into a common language.

Let bodies bolster automated doors' whispered returns.

We tour a gallery.

A museum.

A surgery theatre.

A classroom.

A forest.

A psychiatric ward.

A construction site.

A poem.

Provide labels
to prevent disorientation.

Here, you will make mistakes.

Were a pattern to emerge, it would be a mistake.

To make a mistake organizes an unwanted pattern.

"Here, you will make mistakes" mistakes my message
in favour of an agreeable circumvention.

As a route through the poem, the mistake
envisions me a new body, new hair, limbs reaching.

Eventually, I will ask.

What was taken from you?
What did you take?

My madness is the madness of sequence.

Pause briefly.

Historical facts
fill time.

Performance provides the promise of closure.

You might already imagine leaving, moving
on with your day.

Outside this sentence weather portions a sky.

To begin a tour again somewhere else
threatens to build new rooms, new buildings.

Draw
on shared reference
points
in description.

You stand, now, in the first section.

How will you pass this by?

Will you recognize the face that recognizes
this face?

I rehearse a remarkable occurrence.
My witness, unsaid.

Alone, I step into questioning.
Move beyond explanation.

Rehearse:
greet naturally
rationalize theory
bide between.

A tour situated between two axes: spatial/temporal.

We're still on the ground floor.
Still within architecture's tautology.

Caught between my spoken, my stilled evidence.

Fill air between a modular, an other.
A covered in glass.

A tour's built in the breath.

Exhibit a delayed return.

Rooms become rhymes.

Continuity but an enactment of subtle dissonance.

Stand reflective:

senses vanish
approach language
lapsed unfurling
doubled interior.

The guide is merely the one who follows the tour first.

in following:

Weather distributes floor plans.

No place.

Our bodies held to measurement.

"Are you still there?" we ask ourselves.

We trail the authority of corners, their convergence.

The gesture always beyond.

We, a dissonance beyond witness.

Evenly spaced, signs indicate displayed material.

"Sensations motivate a skin," we reassure ourselves.

We pre-archive experience.

Our lack furnishes a posture.

Tentatively: a position.

We trace the autonomy of corners.

A tension of elements prompts the first step.

A breaking point: the second.

exit strategy

First a leader or "head of the line" is chosen.

Crowd blanks painting to assert a presence
where strips of light display a featureless scene.

Back to front and hardly working. Dust collects
witnesses in echoing corridors. Muffled coughs.

Can't help but step forward among me-first
methodologies. Pangs of past exhibitions.

Public as a stone. Decay creeps coronas
against a plinth. Limbs askew to shore a deficit.

Standing here alone, against another face.
Where stolen goods rework half-felt embraces.

Players line up behind the leader.

Sometimes puppets fake formalism, splay
limbs' routine. Embarrassing the way

words risk delay, prompt action. Works
swerve into resistant objects.

How we bear anxious dialogue, note slogans
in the lineup. And underwater now, drowning

days against a schedule. Diet of warm liquids.
Doctor's advice. The birds too notice this death.

The leader then moves around.

Embrace touches lobotomy. We move
as sensible children mimicking animals.

So motion, left out. Numbers much augmented
in the exchange. Famous faces everywhere.

These playful self-erasures. See the deficit
of encounters border a cry for help.

All the players have to mimic the leader's actions.

Shame of nostalgia as a line demonstrates
duration in its imprecise repetitions.

The machinery of exhaustion and desire shepherds
a relationship. Our hinged movements: survivors.

Any player who fails to follow the leader is out of the game.

A map of possible exits from the collective. The metric with which a body measures the pressure of a solid world.

When only one player remains, that player becomes the leader.

a tour, variously

Depart at regular intervals.

I exhibit rehearsal.
I have seen this face before.

Together, you notice how the cracks in the glass
create it anew in your noticing.

Reorder objects of persuasion.

Did you speak before the tour began?

Did you claim a posture of response?

A voice might change.
From a distance a voice may appear to change.

I see the face of another and recognize a name.

Support structures an unequal encounter.

Name this distance.

You're always on the wrong foot, I might say.

Come closer and see.

Has my narration become cold and inhuman?

Export.
Import.

A portrait gallery of affective absences.

Service
movement.

The narrative trajectory of the tour requires
my motivating force.

How emotionless this recalcitrant model.

I resist the entropy my wander.

Note values.
Face the other.

In weaving lines against the edges of the tour
you draw your likenesses in ink.

Disinterest dictates
indefinite occupancy.

Smudge fingerprint psychologies as you drift on.

Remember is always an absence.
The truth value of becoming falters.

In question only my skin, glancing touches.

Expanses.
Curatorial focal points.

In truth you've visited only ghosts,
frames of our possible convergence.

Reflection of display case aporias impose doubt.

Mistake you to yourself.
Its thrust, your destination.

Patient lenses of the common illusion.

A body poised to produce:
incommensurable ratios
ballasts of presence
removable redundancies.

I pose words above pinned specimens.

Doubts collect.
Twofold axioms cloud.

Nothing moves you to permit a symmetry.

Utterance: a flesh-and-bone matter.

An exterior view and the reorganization of exclusion.

I have done this all before, differently.

Upon a pedestal.

A figure strains in gesture.

Direct attention
case by case.

If I speak of you and I as two
it is because I imagine an amalgam.

Under the spotlight a rose interrogates
                    the conditions of its wilting.

Not a rose, now, but a moment cut from a sentence.

In sequence anything might suggest a resolution.

Without a resolution
                    "not a rose" schedules your brief attention.

"Not a rose" repeats a monotonous presence as exhibition.

Are you fatigued?

A body might be made of many parts.

To hold a posture becomes a labour of enactment.

You and I, both, collect the parts of ourselves
that fail this guise.

At intervals I will query a permission.

Hold open.

A formalist pavilion.

Your particulate response wagers an industry of reception.

A work. A works.
An unearned product of accumulation.

A fiction in singular.

Maintain subtle distance.
Frame nouns.
Note posture.

By degrees or not at all. You and I share a word.

Next:
corroborate
a reasonable balance.

Have I known the archives of ascent?

Have I built my walls too soon?

I must have passed the threshold of concrete lineaments.

I move you on
rehearse an interrogative reflective gaze.

Until someone whispers:

exits open outwards.

in following:

We rehearse a mourning.

We posit a natural world.

This atmospheric wash of spectacle.

Our critical faculties strewn anonymous.

Our discomfort in the bareness of description.

Temporary right now.

How rooms displace their contents.

Two voices would be enough to tour.

Excerpt of our choral balance.

Mimic leaves, touch branches.

Covet immobile roots, rich soil.

A face brightens in response to another.

We're stilled among objects beyond our reach, other voices.

We remember a plan, a map, an alignment of rafters.

Our analogue dislocates the sequence.

Thinking: we constitute a passage.

We collapse and keep time.

atget's interiors

The clock lived into the wall, the chair into the floor. The right contractor extracted gelatin silver prints, lined the basin. Such periods are not sealed, they scan too rapidly and modernisms emerge where furniture once lay. The micropolitics of motes of dust display the brute force of contamination. Being is being, overflow overflow. The end of responsibility and justice welcomed on the brink of tears, laughter in the fermenting groves. Not an avatar of nature, not beyond the hither side. The itinerary designates a florid remonstration.

Who looks to the endpoint of motion. Who stands aside to watch the scene unfold. Movers lifting the possessions of the dead, their worn seats hefted through the open door. No research is rational. The frustrated appearance of a stranger strikes an eye atomic. The logical annexation of habits, wounds insensible. Exasperated riots tear pinholes to a catalogue pitch. The materialist picks a persistent scab. To sense is to expose oneself, to allow a violent chemical light to impress its burnt-white score.

Back against a wall plays at a muscular buttressing. Relationship with a speaking mouth shrinks from volunteering hospitality, however casual. In the red now, accounts overdrawn, the knick-knacks lend credibility to presence. Vast cycles of repair and destruction, idiocies of property. Police study crimes in larger chambers, more expansive atmospheres of weighted scandal. When she saw it she said, I have to have it. This now-broken chair. Pulse races without reason in the evening. The use of music in such situations fills the air, relieves discomfort.

Her theoretical parenthesis capitulates to a demand for rigour where gravity gives way to a flex beyond apprehension. This description becomes furniture music. Neighbours continue to tap tunelessly as the water boils. Calendars betray an orthodox distinction among architectural time, though not without ceding a frivolity to the diptych. Likewise, passageways persuade by degrees. Screens peel from the window, thus we expose ourselves unequally. A passion for lace. Black mould in the corner's skirting. Breathed-in occupant spores. Staircases spiral beyond the gaze, anchor cavities in the gallery.

Advertising syllogisms nest around the weaver-cum-archivist of possessive labours. She presents herself as a face that in turn presents desire. The sleight of hand that supports being must draw from a tucked stash elsewhere. Reduce pressure on the temples. Such incommensurable measures denounce the motivations of a common consciousness. Will she recommend without regard. Such interiority, such economy of rationalism turned to the apology.

Her alphabetical speaks volumes. Commodities compared and contrasted against an abstraction of the market's potential offerings. Hangers-on grasp the radical affirmation of human symmetry. Though when they speak, they speak alone. Cling-film pieces fall to the cutting-room floor. Highways' on- and off-ramps interpolate a hasty journey borne out by keys hung from front-door locks, an unlatched gate. She moves to observe a death as it occurs, though always arrives on the wrong side of the quartet's resolve. Workers monitor the water supply. Zealots drink straight from the well.

Carved entrepreneurial vistas repudiate an implication in the particulate routines of the passenger classes. Uneven production of surplus gestures stimulates speculation among the pigeon witnesses. Baroque companions and mothball comrades who gamble a stain on hand-woven wool rugs. Do her pockets, too, leak on the doormat's untruth. Additives that mediate the metabolism of a coughing quotation cite without appendix. A scatterbrain photography of traumatic encounters with the absent classes. Unremarkable faces behind the scene, among the equipment of past performances.

Without the "now" of standardized speech, the loiterers drag bruised aphorisms. Or so say the lawyers on the courthouse's brutalist concrete steps. Or so say the courthouse's brutalist concrete steps. Either way the difference amounts only to the distance between arrival and departure lounges. Call it documentary, call it eavesdropping, call it the boredom of nostalgia. Feet up, relaxing into the gift economy of composites of real photographs of real horses' mouths.

a tour, variously

I labour to speak as distance mistakes duration.

I, who has begun to transition under your viewership.

Begin in middle
as if continuing previous.

I balance my haptic belonging.

An arrangement of limbs to indicate a possession.

Descriptions bide
between exhibits.

Every effort I have made to restore
the tour to its original state.

One might improvise at this point.

The tour builds its failure into the silences of my patter.

I, anew, an affecting display.

My actions begin to exceed rooms' limits.
In dialogue: perpetual.

I account for a narrative self in question.

I affect my trivial poetics
first as performance.

Texture speech
with decorative.

Am I going around in circles?

No, in repetition I materialize
mistake into the novelty of identity.

Behind each wall an archive of ill at ease.

I will never meet you again.

Labelled jars line wire racks.
            Specimens of an implication.

You need not worry.

I will never meet you again.

A point.
A perusal.
Address audience.

As patterns recede, objects disarray a common perspective.

A narrow route.
An arrow.
Describe error.

You discern a guidebook trajectory.

My voice initiates the collapse of the map's optimism.

The ornament of haphazard ruins that you and I tour.

I recollect the horizon in its dispersal.

An accumulative identity serves adequately.

Monologue now:
mock-up
a tourist attention.

An ornamental shade. A deflection.

You constitute affinity among fabrics,
affect the threshold of mutual enclosure.

Each sentence's failure graphs the following exhibit.

I fray at the edges of each tour's sentence; an unvoiced
sound held by vocalic seams.

Verbose aisles occupy time and distance.

A passage.

Thorough, you indulge my lapse.

Ensure adequate supplies.

Strata, narrowed in on, trip up, or under repair.

To turn a corner, a dissolution anew.

Passing mirrors, I recognize my former absence.

Once unspoken operations reinterpreted through
a conflicted individual multitude.

Keep up.

Unable to wait, now.

The tour limits this moment, separates it from the next.

How to denote a property in dialogue?

A tragedy of errors. Ivy weaves a terrace.

Must I attempt an art
or reveal the refraction anew?

When will exit signs accumulate a vitalism of my escape?

Preserve
head space.

Who responds to the mirror and its ever-increasing absence?

You tour but my echo.

in following:

We mistake gestures for a familiar face.

Empirically, we are told, another.

We note each moment as it passes.

We render contingency remarkable.

Our exteriors in unison.

Dominated by straight lines, minimalist gravities.

The clarity of a didactic body stands before us, lips open.

We break pamphlets down to constituent elements.

An open invitation.

A friendship.

We misread leisure for influence.

Letters and pulp fall sweaty to the floor.

A swiftly closing door.

theory of rooms

Index:

Body of objects' limits

House without rooms, but toy models of rooms

Framework detail

Possessive fold

Drywall premises

Topography of closured lengths

Table to delimit oblique

Marginal exhibition of flexibility

Bodies' geometric lack

Apartment in singular

Parallel life

Conflict in the mine

Topology of the unspoken

Network of measurable surfaces

Absorptive line

Replica, in case

Manifesto species

Plausible coalition of material

Column without figures

Threadbare desire

Flexible methodology

Commerce among minerals

Face-to-face encounter

Artery chalk

Building without recourse

Plans delineated within and without

Decorative rejections

Two dimensions as painted

Plastic contour of the conditional

Ecstatic schemas of theory

Asymmetrical plurality

Politics of proximate equation

Procedures of decadent flexure

Concretized sensation

Inevitable ownership delays

Accreted anxiety

Column without words

Tacked gathering of fabric

Wall's horizontal score

Room buried under rooms

Strategies of accumulation

This is a building theory of rooms.
Symmetry to formulate inhabitants.
Arms too, framed in cloth excuses.

This is a room for theory building.
Installation to misguide a relationship.
Coarse fibres, scheduled in warmth.

This is a theory building rooms.
Material to recuperate a tenuous encounter.
The saying and the unsaid, built at the same time.

Rooms with furniture inside.
Inside buildings. Buildings repeat in a city.
Food left on table rewrites a presence.

A room refuses help. Chairs remain, and later.

Animals who live in maps of forests.
Forests shaped like rooms in building.
Animals labour to expand the boundary.

Rooms of forests on another coast.
Buildings recycle a muscular tension.
From a distance it looks the same.

A builder selects theme and locality.
Vacant units.
Fur grows thick to hide a building.
Denounce enclosure.

A note towards a foundation:
revolution will not dislocate joints of concrete operation.

Limited space to build buildings adds rooms to other buildings.
Grey clouds circle the city, grow taut and feral frames.

From need to room, the power to room.

From character of thought, a democratic rest.

A self's motion to construct a record.

Fragile counting animals, their utilitarian motifs.

Which rots, which wood and iron.

Composed in secular mastery.

Deferrals accumulate above one another.

To redecorate a patterned belonging.

Advice:

Lay out the ground lines the length and breadth of the monument proposed.

Collect foliage for the upper tier, browned leaves for flooring.

What remains ever exterior to thought is thought.

Lay bare the concrete while still damp.

Place visionary on paper, anticipate business to come.

The room does not exist before revealing itself.

Curve and scale may lead us to false impressions.

Surveil the animal complacencies beyond the door.

A forum models a proportionate citizenry.

Retain the excess, motivate a corrective.

Count the legs of the chair before an occupation.

Do not allow negativity to presuppose a body only to remove it.

Fortify with gravity walls, the cantilevered embankments.

The continuous voice does not still at any boundary or definite place.

Distrust a rabid architect, his accountant.

Figures carved in bark require a corroborative word.

Loose the jury among the beasts to discern a common scale.

Extremities of progress remain ever unapparent.

Discredit those braces which too easily carry their load.

Remember, adjectives are economic.

In discord and concord, an intermixture of support.

Lintel to builders: the units, as designed,

fulfill an unspoken promise, a lapsed faith.

The solid volume of yelps' waves.

(a consensus of lived experience)

Instigate postplanning stages of investment.

(or otherwise assembled language)

Weary when seated, a subject repositions.
Style beckons remonstrance.

Thus liberal rooms still layer.
A building still movement.
Windows still a wall.
Still diffuse areas, mobile sectors.

Canines at the ready during speech.
Wallpaper affixed to replicate the de-escalation.

Suppose autonomy. Suppose a hibernation.
A market-adjusted room to breathe.
Motivated by an impossible exchange.
A room impassable. Reconciled in miniature.

Once horizontal withdraws, the work varies access.
Vanishing point delegates a private scale.
Margins trace transitional infestations.

The gravity of solace resists environmental torque.
Interstitial potential. Converge upon an irreducible.
Particulars of plural enfoldings.

Reason generates relation.
Violent affronts built among shame. Follows:
utility, material. By fine migratory lines.

Animal rooms precarious among livable absences.
Movies and a disinterested insulation.
Closed against previous interior.
Revolt or bed down.

Costs of Construction:

Cost of breathlessness

Cost of sand

Cost of aggregate

Cost of making by hand

Cost of making by machine

Cost of deposit

Cost of the ethical encounter

Cost of form construction

Cost of moulding

Cost of degraded trust

Cost of fortifications

Cost of retaining walls

Cost of foundation

Cost of lining tunnels

Cost of reinforcement

Cost of ornamental work

Cost of exposure

a tour, variously

As you look towards exits, you begin to construct yourselves
in the past tense of the poem's touring.

I begin to overlap tours as an elaboration
of a self anew.

Descent, or another spatializing metaphor.

Define an ending.
Provide closure.

Betrayal were I to impose an autobiographical
backwards glance.

Register
transient belonging.

As you traverse beyond rooms you will notice
and forget to notice.

Register
contingencies
exigencies
redundancies.

Parallel lines gesture outwards towards a natural
conclusion.

Shelf life of a monologue in motion.

Come
this far, no farther.

You open your eyes towards a burgeoning light.

Permissive, or an offstage rebuttal.

A patterned object in multiple coordinates
your waning gaze.

When does change fall into deception?

And did I possess the faculties to ask
this question earlier?

When does change fall into deception?

When the viewer looks away.

As you enter this room, remember
exhibitions past.

Telegraph the end.

You and I, who have been through so much.
Or rather so many.

Baroque permutations curate exhibition's schedule.

My time disorders and disorders.

When you emerge into a new world, you will rebuild
this tour to explain how you were born fully grown.

Traced in outline, you might recognize your habits
as the static sculptures of another's attention.

I, long gone, then cannot, will not, catalogue this elapse again.

Indicate eras
but
always
contextualize
scale.

My emptiness affixes tour's ultimatum as identity. Though
I have moved past these roped-off spaces.

Thank you in advance for letting me go.

Perform friendly
final thoughts.

Provide
reflective

directions.

Perhaps, though, I have become enamoured with a posture.

I might offer an apology in lieu of a next step.

Begotten accordances

Gift-shop condolences.

You, clearly passionate, adopt a resolution
perfectly coordinated to fashion.

To meditate on an emergent design
flowing outwards without regard.

I would hesitate a commotion.

I would gesture beyond painted walls.

A proposal: forget the tour.

Abandon the poem to the void of past.

Wager a future unprecedented.

Who might you be now?

As I depart to renew a cycle
                I reread your faces and remember.

In a gaze an admission of soft tissue.

You may destroy me now.

I am not she who toured before.

in following:

In answer we assimilate the question into a rehearsal of return.

In departure, we propose a multiple "I" to reconcile our division.

Confronted with inertia's authority we acquiesce.

Opaque sculptures of memory.

Our hungers multiple, preserved.

Museums of light portion indiscriminate archives.

Disorientation labels us perpetual tourists.

Such colours exteriorize a surplus.

Our variations on a theme: a meander.

Memory proves our unreliable guide.

We tour variously.

We who initiated the tour's entrance.

Stares to resist the inevitable resolution.

If only a group, or the desire to speak beyond ourselves.

notes and acknowledgments

The Emmanuel Levinas epigraph is a slight modification of a sentence in *Totality and Infinity: An Essay on Exteriority*, translated by Alphonso Lingis.

Information for Docents is a pamphlet produced by the National Collection for Fine Arts in 1974, accessed via the HathiTrust Digital Library.

"exit strategy" makes use of text from the *Wikipedia* article for the game follow-the-leader.

Earlier versions of some of these poems were published in *7seconds, BafterC, Cough, CV2, Dandelion, The Ex-Puritan, filling Station, Rampike, The Trinity Review, White Wall Review*, and *The Windsor Review*. Thank you to the editors of each.

A section of "Theory of Rooms" was published as a chapbook by above/ground press as *Theory of Rooms*. Thank you to rob mclennan.

The first poem of the "a tour, variously" suite was set as an art song titled "Uncertain Property" by composer Adam Scime and performed in Vancouver as part of the (Art) Song Lab in 2015.

Thank you to Phinder Dulai and Catriona Strang for editorial guidance and support.

This manuscript received Ontario Arts Council Writer's Reserve funding.

Thank you, always, to Kit MacNeil, whose encouragement and championing of this book and support of me made it finally possible.

Drew McEwan is the author of the poetry collections *Repeater* and *If Pressed*. She works as an educator and researcher with a focus on mad, disability, queer, and trans rhetoric.